When Royals Wore Ruffles

A Funny & Fashionable Alphabet!

WRITTEN BY CHESLEY McLAREN AND PAMELA JABER

ILLUSTRATED BY CHESLEY McLAREN

schwartz & wade books · new york

A IS FOR ATTitude! AN Absolute Must

It's not the size of your bow, your mother's pearls, or parading about in high, high heels.
It's the spring in your step and your turned-up nose—

that's Attitude, Attitude, Attitude!

All through history, stylish ladies and fashionable men never left home without it.

B IS FOR BUSTLES

With piles of fabric bunched up on their behinds, ladies in the 1800s sported a new look with the invention of the bustle. It gave them a very, *very* curvy shape. The bustle, which tied around the waist, was made of stiff ruffles, pads and sometimes even metal.

and the BUSTLE beyond BELIEF!

Over the years, the bustle changed shape, getting bigger and bigger until it finally went out of style in the early 1900s.

But even today you can still buy a padded "fanny"!

The most magnificent bustle of all had a music box hidden inside, which blasted out "God Save the Queen," the British national anthem, whenever the lady wearing it sat down! It was a fun souvenir created to celebrate Queen Victoria's fiftieth anniversary as England's ruler in 1887.

C IS FOR Couture

A couture (coo-TOOR) dress is one of a kind and made especially for you.

It can take yards and yards of fabric, hundreds of rolls of lace and thousands of feathers, flowers and jewels.

And it can take months to sew, weigh up to 300 pounds and cost as much as a house!

Now, THAT'S a DRESS!

Very few ladies own a couture dress, but learn to sew, and you can make your own.

D IS FOR DRESS

as in "Little Black Dress"

Black was declared fashionable in 1926 when the famous designer Coco Chanel created the "little black dress."

Before this time, black was only appropriate for a lady when she was mourning the death of a family member. And now black is what lots of people wear ALL the time—funny how it's become glamorous!

An LBD (little black dress) is considered a must for every lady's closet.

E IS FOR THE EMPIRE, THE EMPRESS

Napoleon, the French emperor, took his new wife, Josephine, to Italy to meet his family in 1796. They were shocked and embarrassed by this lady from Paris, who appeared to be wearing nothing but a flimsy nightie!

and the INFAMOUS DRESS!

Josephine's dress style was called Empire (ahm-PEER). It was simple, sheer and very daring for its day.

Napoleon's idea of style was quite different from his wife's. He wanted more, more, MORE: more fabric, more fur, more gold, more EVERYTHING. And to force the ladies to wear more, he even had all the fireplaces in the palace closed up. IT WAS FREEZING!

The Empire look is still very stylish today.

F IS FOR THE FLAPPERS WHO ROARED THROUGH THE 20S

How to do the Charleston: Flap your arms like a baby bird and knock your knees together!

Off with the petticoats and up with the hems!

This was a scandalous way to dress, for it showed off a lady's legs in public—unheard of!

For two hundred years, legs had been hidden—even PIANO legs were covered.

These modern girls of the 1920s were called flappers. Draped in ropes of pearls, feathers and fringe, they flipped for the new dance craze, the Charleston.

G is for Go-Go Boots!

The 1960s ~ A Fashion Revolution!

The MOD look invaded America on a British model named Twiggy, who was an icon of the Mod generation and wore a miniskirt, fishnet tights, white lipstick and shiny white go-go boots.

Overnight everyone was going mod: kids, moms, even the president's wife! People went berserk for the Beatles and learned to dance the twist.

How to do the twist: Twist your body back and forth (like you're drying off your backside with a towel) while grinding the ball of your foot on the floor. Fun, isn't it?

H IS FOR HIGH HATS AND

The higher the hat, and the higher the hair, the higher your status in society.

In the 1400s, hats reached skyscraper heights.

Ladies wore cone-shaped hats called hennins.

Hennins kept getting taller and taller until servants were required to follow behind the ladies with pitchforks . . . just to hold up their hats!

Hair-Raising Heights!

Hairdos went totally over the top in the 1700s, when ladies had to hang their heads out of their carriage windows to sit down.

Growing up to three feet high with the help of plaster and wigs, hairdos were adorned with plumes, jewels, birds, butterflies, vegetables and, it's been said, even a ship!

It took hours and hours to build these creations. Ladies rarely washed their hair or their wigs. Often the wigs became home to many creepy crawlers.

I IS FOR AN ILLEGAL INTRUDER
THE WIG SNATCHER

With all the jewels in their wigs, ladies became the target of the dreaded WIG SNATCHERS.

Robbers would sneak up behind a lady's coach, cut a hole in the back, snatch the wig—and off they'd run!

I-YI-YI! Who knew being fashionable could be so dangerous?

J IS FOR JEWELS

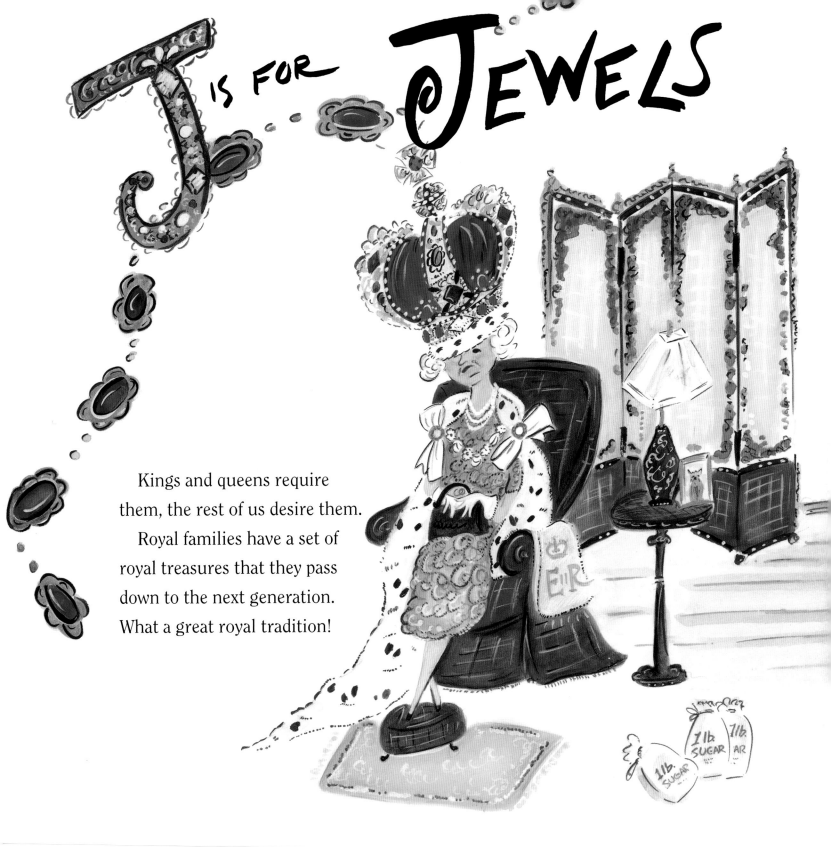

Kings and queens require them, the rest of us desire them.

Royal families have a set of royal treasures that they pass down to the next generation. What a great royal tradition!

The Imperial State Crown of England has 2,868 diamonds, 273 pearls, 17 sapphires, 11 emeralds and 5 rubies and is worn once a year by Queen Elizabeth at the State Opening of Parliament.

All those jewels weigh a lot—almost three pounds. That's like wearing three bags of sugar on your head!

Since the crown is so heavy, Queen Elizabeth often practices wearing it for a few hours before appearing in public.

K is for the **KING'S KNICKERS** and **KNEES**

The Peacock Age was a time in history when the gentlemen outshone the ladies in fashion. In the 1600s, men strutted their stuff in furs, frills and even heels.

Knee-length pants were designed to show off legs and, in the case of the French King Louis XIV, his magnificent red heels! The red heels were a sign of nobility and were worn only by the king and his court.

L IS FOR THE LEGS THAT THE LADY Lassoed!

When Katharine Wright, the sister of the Wright brothers (who invented the flying machine, or airplane), got ready for her first flight, she discovered a teensy problem: her skirt. Enormous full skirts were the style of the day, so she tied a rope around her skirt just above her ankles to keep it from flying all over the place. And then she hobbled on board.

Supposedly, a famous French designer was inspired by her look and declared it the new style in the early 1900s. The hobble skirt was so narrow at the bottom, a lady could hardly walk. She just hobbled along . . . or fell over!

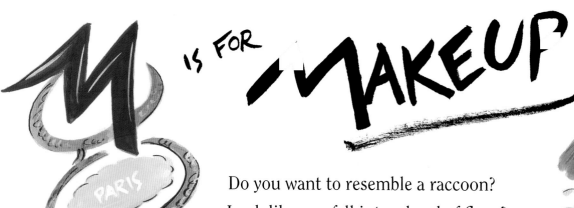

M IS FOR MAKEUP

Do you want to resemble a raccoon?
Look like you fell into a bowl of flour?
Certainly not!
But everyone has their own idea of beauty,
and using makeup is an idea that's ancient.

Cleopatra got her red lipstick
by crushing red beetles, ants and
finally fish scales, which added a
nice shimmery quality. Yum!

In the 1700s, well-to-do men and women globbed on layers
of thick, white lead makeup, even though they knew it was
poisonous and could make them sick. Yikes!
In the late 1800s, it was fashionable to look pale and pasty—
drinking a tall glass of vinegar did the trick. Yuck!

N IS FOR THE NOSE

Very few have the privilege of being called a nose—also known as a perfumer.

The requirement for the job is an EXTREMELY keen sense of smell.

Often perfumers spend years concocting the perfect scent, blending oils from flowers, spices, fruits and herbs.

People have always loved perfume. The Egyptians believed that soothing smells healed illness. In the 1500s, Europeans had no running water to wash with, so they doused themselves in perfume to hide unpleasant odors. Today we use it just to smell sweet.

But user BEWARE: Too much can cause violent sneezing, coughing or even gagging!

The trick: Spray the perfume lightly into the air and sashay through the mist.

O IS FOR OUCH!

Oh, the pain we put ourselves through to be beautiful! Imagine this: You're dressing for a dance in the 1500s. You're SQUEEZED into a contraption called a corset, made of whalebones or steel rods. You're pinched and tugged and laced up tight. You couldn't possibly eat—you can barely BREATHE! But the good news is: You now have a stylish, tiny thirteen-inch waist! (That's smaller than a grown man's NECK!) The bad news is: You'll probably faint or break a rib before the dance is over. . . .

P IS FOR YOUR POCKETS

Before ladies carried purses, they hauled stuff around in their pockets.

But not little pockets like we have today; no, these pockets were HUGE! In the mid-1600s, the pockets were tied around the waist and hidden under the skirt. The skirts had big slashes in the side so a lady could reach in. It was a little like dragging two laundry bags around!

One big problem: The pockets sometimes came untied and your belongings were strewn all over the street.

All proper young ladies learned to sew. Pockets were a perfect thing to practice on, since your mistakes couldn't be seen.

Q IS FOR Questionable STYLES

Since the 1970s, fashion has produced some pretty, well, questionable looks. Starting with Punk in the seventies, we ripped and shredded everything we wore and then put it all back together again with safety pins and tape. And we had stiff Mohawk hairstyles. In the eighties, Punk was remade into the Gothic look. The Goth uniform included lots of makeup, and Victorian styles like corsets and petticoats, and most of our clothes were black. Then, in the early 1990s, Grunge gave us that just-rolled-out-of-bed look. We wore raggedy jeans, flannel shirts and long, greasy hair.

R IS FOR THE ROYALS— RUFFLED, ROUND AND Rich!

The stylish ruffled collar called the ruff was worn only by the upper class. Ruffs got so big and stiff during the 1500s that royals had to use special elongated silverware to eat! Starch was discovered at that time, which meant even stiffer, wider, huger ruffs—so enormous that some of them had to be supported by wire attached from behind.

As far as round and rich goes, royalty has always indulged itself in all the fancy foods it can afford (a LOT!). Henry VIII died with a waist measuring fifty-four inches.

S is for Shoes, Shoes

SATIN SLIPPER

The platform has been around for centuries; the satin slipper has been the ladies' choice since the 1700s; and Mary Janes have been a girl's first party shoe since the 1900s.

MARY JANE

PLATFORMS

The granny boot got its name from Grandma's laced-up boots; the Greek sandal was made from scraps of leather; the Turkish slipper was curled up for no apparent reason; and the riding boot is always stylish, even without a horse!

and More Shoes

GREEK SANDAL

TURKISH SLIPPER

FIRST HIGH HEEL

GRANNY BOOT

RIDING BOOT

And then there was the first high heel.
To look magnificent at the French court, Catherine de Médicis, the Queen of France, had the wooden soles taken off her shoes and replaced with slim four-inch heels—the first high-heeled shoes! De Médicis married Henry II in 1533 at the age of fourteen, and she was a very stylish lady. What she wore set trends around the world.

T IS FOR TEETERING about TOWN on your Toes

Venice was a bumpy, muddy city back in the 1500s, and tall shoes were needed to rise above all that muck. Worn over a slipper, a chopine was a wooden shoe on a platform. Only, these platforms were TOWERING: Some of them were thirty inches high.

Decorated with jewels, painted with gold or covered in velvet or leather, they were EXTREME. Height became a status symbol, and all over Europe, women reached such dizzy new heights that they needed servants to help them stand (and MOVE). After too many accidents, chopines went out of style.

U IS FOR UNMENTIONABLES

Ladies' Girdles

The girdle squeezed the corset out of popularity in the mid-1900s. You yanked and pulled and squished yourself into this thick rubber underwear to get the perfect hourglass shape.

When the first nylons appeared in New York stores in the 1930s, people went CRAZY, and 72,000 pairs were sold on the FIRST DAY! (Ladies loved them because they were glamorous, looked like silk and, best of all, were inexpensive.) The fabric nylon was named after the cities New York and London.

"Unmentionables"—from corsets to brassieres—used to be worn only underneath our clothes. Not anymore! Sometimes they ARE our clothes.

V IS FOR VANITY & VERY HIGH VOLTAGE

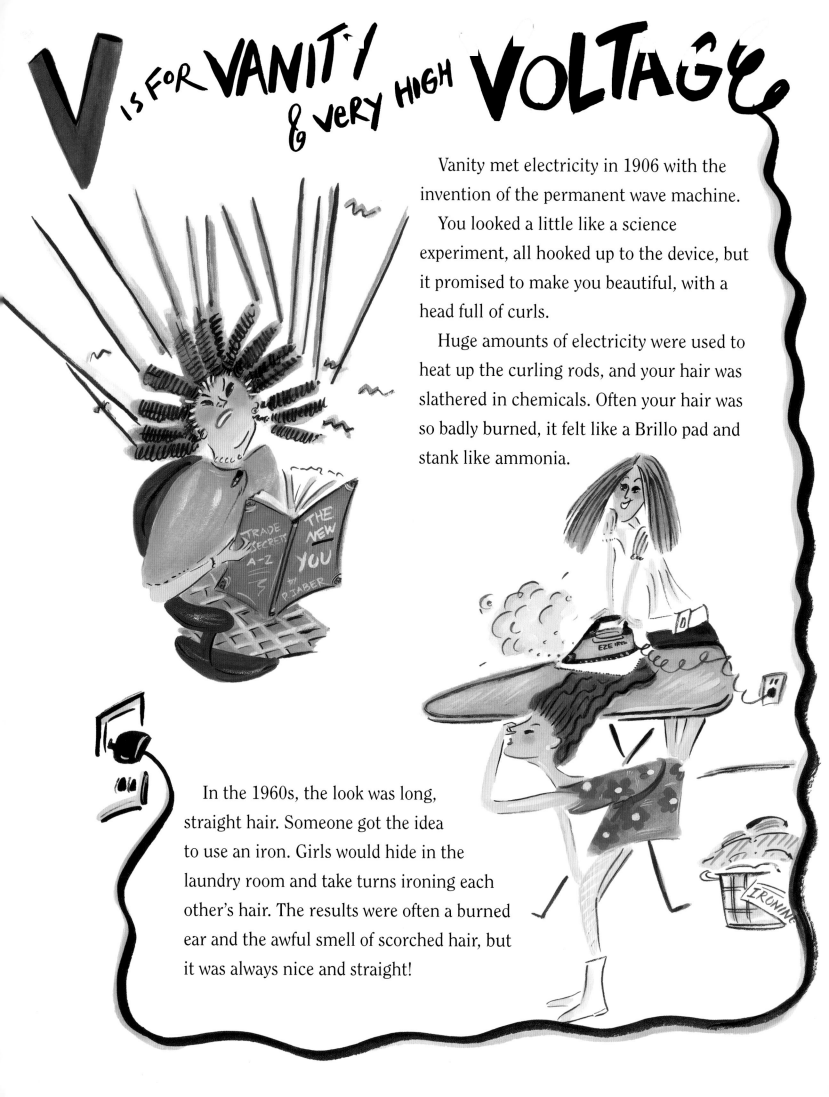

Vanity met electricity in 1906 with the invention of the permanent wave machine.

You looked a little like a science experiment, all hooked up to the device, but it promised to make you beautiful, with a head full of curls.

Huge amounts of electricity were used to heat up the curling rods, and your hair was slathered in chemicals. Often your hair was so badly burned, it felt like a Brillo pad and stank like ammonia.

In the 1960s, the look was long, straight hair. Someone got the idea to use an iron. Girls would hide in the laundry room and take turns ironing each other's hair. The results were often a burned ear and the awful smell of scorched hair, but it was always nice and straight!

W IS FOR WHO? WHAT? WHEN? and WHERE?

Sometimes fashion happens by accident. . . . England's Earl of Spencer was reclining by the fire. The tails of his coat got a little too close and burst into flames. He was fine, but his jacket was not—all that was left was the singed, tailless coat.

Voilà—the spencer coat was born.

The style spread like wildfire in the late 1700s!

BEFORE

AFTER

X is for eXtraORDINARY and totally eXtreme

It has been said that history repeats itself.

Lacroix

Chalayan

Watanabe

On the runways of today, do you think these styles might be the modern versions of the past? Could the bubble be the new bustle? The chandelier headdress the new high hat? The huge ruffle the new ruff?

Y IS FOR YOU AND YOUR VERY OWN style AND

Ribbon
MADE IN PARIS
-SILK-

Z IS FOR THE Zany WORLD

As you've seen, some styles were hilarious, some were lucky accidents and some were just plain silly.

OF FASHION

One thing's for sure:
Style is not just the ribbons or the bows.
It's the spring in your step and your turned-up nose.
Now head out the door, and don't forget your

Attitude!